Searchlight BOOKS™

What's Amazing about Space?

Exploring Black Holes

Laura Hamilton Waxman

Lerner Publications Company
Minneapolis

► For the scientists in the family: Buddy, Momo, and Caleb
The author would like to thank Dr. Monwhea Jeng for his help with the preparation of this book.

Lerner Publications Company
A division of Lerner Publishing Group, Inc.
241 First Avenue North
Minneapolis, MN 55401 U.S.A.

Website address: www.lernerbooks.com

Library of Congress Cataloging-in-Publication Data

Waxman, Laura Hamilton.
    Exploring black holes / by Laura Hamilton Waxman.
        p.   cm. — (Searchlight books™—What's amazing about space?)
    Includes index.
    ISBN 978-0-7613-5442-0 (lib. bdg. : alk. paper)
    1. Black holes (Astronomy)—Juvenile literature. I. Title.
QB843.B55W39 2012
523.8'875—dc22   2010035378

Manufactured in the United States of America
1 – DP – 7/15/11

Contents

Chapter 1

A GREAT SPACE
MYSTERY ... page 4

Chapter 2

BLACK HOLES UP CLOSE ... page 9

Chapter 3

FALLING INTO A BLACK HOLE ... page 17

Chapter 4

BIRTH OF A BLACK HOLE ... page 22

Chapter 5

STUDYING BLACK HOLES ... page 30

Glossary • 38
Learn More about Black Holes • 39
Index • 40

A GREAT SPACE MYSTERY

Black holes are a mystery of outer space. People can see stars, planets, and other objects in the sky. But black holes are invisible. We cannot see them.

This artwork shows what a black hole might look like if we could see it. Can you find the black hole?

Astronomers study outer space. These scientists can look at planets and stars. But they can't look at black holes. That's why black holes are such mysteries.

An astronomer adjusts a giant telescope. Astronomers use telescopes to study outer space.

What Is a Black Hole?

A black hole isn't really a hole. It is an area in space with very strong gravity. Gravity is a force that pulls objects together. Earth's gravity keeps us from floating away. We can jump off the ground. But Earth's gravity pulls us back down.

Gravity makes this parachuter fall back to Earth.

A black hole's gravity is much stronger than Earth's. Its gravity is stronger than anything in the universe. The universe is all of outer space.

An artist created this picture of a black hole. The black hole is surrounded by stars, dust, and gas.

Anything that comes near a black hole quickly gets sucked into it.

A black hole's gravity pulls in any object that gets too close. Anything that falls into a black hole disappears. Even light cannot escape. That's why a black hole is invisible. It gives off no light.

Chapter 2

BLACK HOLES UP CLOSE

Objects have different strengths of gravity. Earth's gravity is stronger than the Moon's. The Sun's gravity is stronger than Earth's. What causes this difference?

Earth and the Moon both have gravity. Which one has stronger gravity?

YOU COULD FIT MORE THAN
1 MILLION EARTH-SIZED PLANETS
INTO THE SUN!

Differences in Gravity

Mass creates gravity. Mass is how much stuff an object is made of. Objects with lots of mass have strong gravity. The Sun has more mass than Earth. That's why the Sun's gravity is stronger.

What Makes a Black Hole?

Black holes have at least three times more mass than the Sun. The largest black holes may have billions of times more mass.

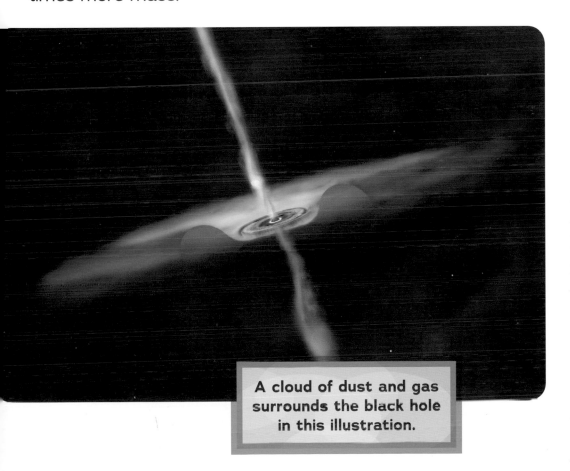

A cloud of dust and gas surrounds the black hole in this illustration.

The Sun is huge. More than one million planets Earth's size could fit inside of it. But a black hole's mass is packed into a single point in space. Astronomers call this point the singularity.

The singularity's gravity creates the black hole.

A black hole's singularity is
very small. It's even smaller
than a pencil's tip!

The singularity is smaller than the tip of a pencil.
Some scientists think it takes up no space at all. That's
hard to imagine. Even scientists have a hard time
understanding it.

Parts of a Black Hole

The singularity lies at the center of a black hole. Gravity is the strongest there. Anything that comes too close to it falls into the black hole.

This photo shows the galaxy Centaurus A. Scientists believe a huge black hole lies at the center of the galaxy.

The event horizon is shown in the center of this drawing of a black hole.

All around the singularity is an area where gravity is very strong. The outer edge of this area is called the event horizon. Any object that crosses the event horizon cannot escape the black hole. The object disappears.

Gravity outside the event horizon is still very strong. It tugs on the gas, the dust, and the stars around it. These objects circle around the black hole at great speeds. The pull of the black hole's gravity grows weaker farther out in space.

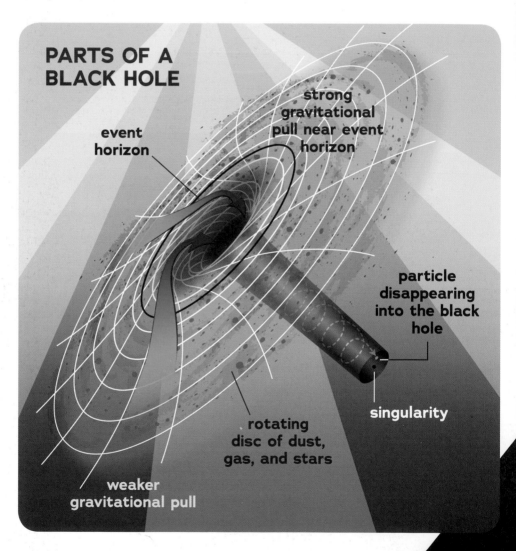

PARTS OF A BLACK HOLE

event horizon

strong gravitational pull near event horizon

particle disappearing into the black hole

singularity

rotating disc of dust, gas, and stars

weaker gravitational pull

Chapter 3

FALLING INTO A BLACK HOLE

What would it feel like to fall into a black hole? No one has ever visited one. The nearest black holes are too far away from Earth. And no person or spacecraft could survive a black hole's gravity. Even so, astronomers have ideas about what might happen.

Do you see the material being pulled into this black hole?

A Giant Waterfall

Imagine a river rushing toward a giant waterfall. Picture yourself floating on that river. The water moves faster as you get closer to the waterfall's edge.

This giant waterfall is in South America.

Once you get too close, you can't turn back. The pull of the river is too strong. Soon you plunge down into the waterfall. That might be what it's like to fall into a black hole.

Astronomers have found a black hole at the center of this nearby galaxy *(lower left)*.

Stretched Thin

You wouldn't last long inside a black hole. Imagine that you fell in feetfirst. Gravity would tug harder on your feet than your head. You would be stretched out like a strand of spaghetti. Then the gravity would rip you into many pieces.

Something pulled into a black hole would be stretched out like these pasta strands.

Deep Inside

No one knows what happens deep inside a black hole. Most astronomers believe that whatever falls into one adds to the singularity's mass. Some astronomers think black holes could be tunnels to other universes.

This is how one artist imagined a black hole.

Chapter 4

BIRTH OF A BLACK HOLE

The universe may have billions of black holes. Where did they all come from?

Can you pick out where the black holes might be in this space photo?

BLACK HOLES FORM FROM LARGE,
DYING STARS. THIS LARGE STAR
IS NAMED ANTARES.

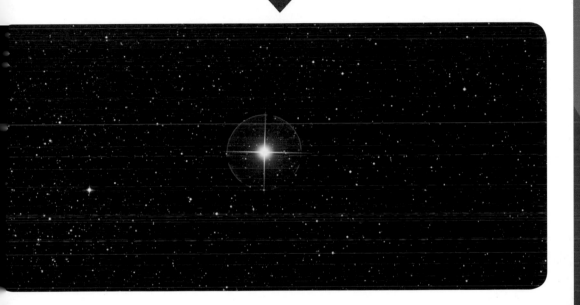

Starting out as Stars

Astronomers think most black holes are stellar. Stellar
black holes form from large, dying stars. The Sun is a
star. But it is a medium-sized star. Stars that form black
holes have at least ten times more mass than the Sun.

Stars surround a black hole in this artwork.

From Star to Black Hole

Stars burn hydrogen gas. Over time, they use up this fuel. They die when they run out of it.

A large star explodes as it dies. The explosion is called a supernova. Some of the star blasts off into space. What's left behind has at least three times more mass than the Sun. That mass shrinks down to a single point. This point forms a new black hole.

**This photo shows
a blast wave from a
supernova.**

Monster Black Holes

Astronomers believe that much larger black holes exist. Scientists call them supermassive black holes. Their mass is millions or billions of times that of the Sun.

This photo shows a supermassive black hole.

Astronomers are not sure how a supermassive black hole forms. It may start out as a stellar black hole. Over time, it sucks up stars, gas, and dust. Slowly, it grows into a monster black hole.

The bright yellow at the center of this drawing is a supermassive black hole.

Or a supermassive black hole may form from many black holes. One black hole sucks up other black holes over time. Or it may form from a huge cloud of gas that forms into a singularity.

An artist has shown two black holes coming together. Scientists believe some giant black holes may have formed this way.

Scientists think that supermassive black holes lie at the center of most galaxies. The Sun is part of our galaxy, the Milky Way. Astronomers believe a huge black hole lies at the center of our galaxy too. But Earth is much too far away to fall into it.

This photo shows an explosion at the center of the Milky Way. A supermassive black hole may lie there.

Chapter 5

STUDYING BLACK HOLES

Hundreds of years ago, scientists asked a question. What would happen if an object had overpowering gravity? The scientists were John Mitchell and Pierre-Simon LaPlace. Their question led to the idea of black holes.

This drawing shows scientist Pierre-Simon LaPlace. How did he help in discovering black holes?

Starting to Solve a Mystery

In the early 1900s, scientist Albert Einstein studied and wrote about gravity. Many scientists read his famous ideas. One of them was Karl Schwarzchild. Schwarzchild used Einstein's ideas to figure out how black holes might work.

Scientists Albert Einstein (top) and Karl Schwarzchild (bottom) helped find out how black holes work.

Still, no one had proof that black holes were real. Most scientists thought they were just an idea. That changed in the 1970s. Astronomers found ways to search for black holes. But how do they look for something they can't see?

This drawing shows a black spot in space. Could this be a sign of a black hole?

X-ray Vision

Astronomers believe that a black hole heats up the gas and the dust that circles it. The heated gas and dust gives off light and energy. X-rays are one type of this energy. Astronomers find black holes by looking for X-rays.

X-rays are coming out of a giant black hole in this artist's image. People cannot see X-rays. Astronomers use special equipment to find them in space.

A star circles a black hole in this artist's drawing.

Circling Stars

Astronomers also watch star movement. Often two stars circle each other in space. Sometimes one star becomes a black hole. The other star keeps circling the black hole. Stars also circle supermassive black holes. So astronomers hunt for stars that are circling something invisible.

Black Hole Hunters in Space

Powerful telescopes on Earth help astronomers search for stars near black holes. Telescopes make distant objects look bigger and closer. Telescopes make stars look brighter and clearer.

This powerful telescope sits atop a mountain in Hawaii.

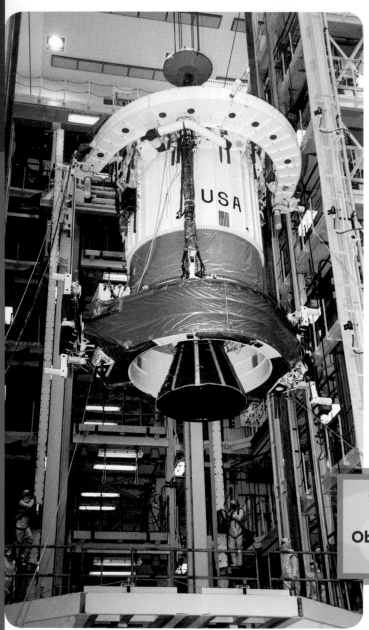

Telescopes in space also allow scientists to search for X-rays. A telescope aboard the Chandra X-ray Observatory left Earth in 1999. The Chandra is a spacecraft that helps scientists find black holes.

Scientists work on the Chandra X-ray Observatory before its launch in 1999.

Astronomers plan to send new telescopes into space to study black holes. The NuSTAR telescopes will be even more powerful than the one aboard the Chandra. And a telescope aboard the International X-ray Observatory will search for very old black holes. These tools may help astronomers learn more about the mystery of black holes.

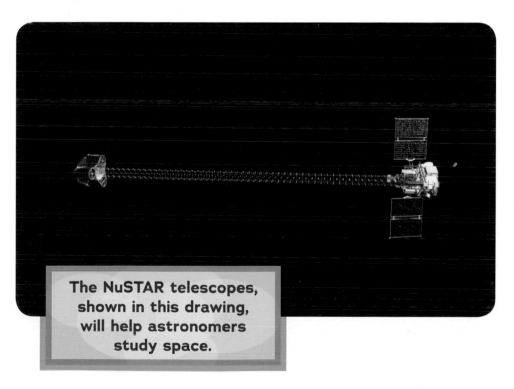

The NuSTAR telescopes, shown in this drawing, will help astronomers study space.

Glossary

astronomer: a scientist who studies outer space

event horizon: the outer edge of a black hole. Anything that crosses the event horizon cannot escape a black hole.

galaxy: a large grouping of stars

gravity: a force that pulls objects together

invisible: unable to be seen

mass: the amount of stuff that makes up an object

singularity: the point at the center of a black hole

stellar: from or having to do with stars

supermassive: extremely large

supernova: a large, dying star that has exploded

telescope: an instrument that makes faraway objects appear bigger and closer

universe: all of outer space

X-ray: one type of energy given off by the heat and the dust that circle a black hole

Learn More about Black Holes

Books

Parker, Katie. *Black Holes*. New York: Marshall Cavendish Benchmark, 2010. This book is a great resource for readers looking for further information on black holes.

Than, Ker. *Black Holes*. New York: Children's Press, 2010. Learn more about black holes and how they form.

Vogt, Gregory L. *Stars*. Minneapolis: Lerner Publications Company, 2010. Readers can learn all about stars, including how they form black holes.

Young, J. E. *Horror in Space*. New York: Graphic Universe, 2011. Your choices help reveal the plot in this interactive space adventure.

Websites

Ask an Astronomer for Kids!: Black Holes
http://coolcosmos.ipac.caltech.edu/cosmic_kids/AskKids/blackholes.shtml
An astronomer answers questions for kids about black holes.

Black Hole Rescue!
http://spaceplace.nasa.gov/en/kids/blackhole/index.shtml
Come to this website for facts, photos, activities, and games about black holes.

Black Holes
http://www.kidsastronomy.com/black_hole.htm
This site helps kids understand how a black hole works.

Index

astronomers, 5, 12, 17, 21, 23,
  26–27, 29, 32–35, 37

Earth, 6–7, 9–10, 12, 17, 29, 35–36

event horizon, 15–16

galaxies, 29

gravity, 6–10, 14–17, 20, 30–31

hydrogen gas, 24

mass, 10–12, 21, 23, 25–26

Moon, 9

planets, 4–5, 12

singularity, 12–15, 21, 28

stars, 4–5, 16, 23–25, 27, 34–35

Sun, 9–12, 23, 25–26, 29

supernova, 25

universe, 7, 21–22

X-rays, 33, 36

Photo Acknowledgments

The images in this book are used with the permission of: © Chris Butler/Photo Researchers, Inc.,
p. 4; © Sandy Huffaker/Getty Images, p. 5; © Dmitrijs Gerciks/Dreamstime.com, p. 6; © Lynette
Cook/Photo Researchers, Inc., p. 7; © Victor de Schwanberg/Photo Researchers, Inc., p. 8; © Digital
Vision/Getty Images, p. 9; © Stocktrek Images/Getty Images, pp. 10, 27; NASA/CXC/M. Weiss,
pp. 11, 17, 19; © Shigemi Numazawa/Atlas Photo Bank/Photo Researchers, Inc., p. 12; © Simon Krzic/
Dreamstime.com, p. 13; © Science Source/Photo Researchers, Inc., p. 14; © David A. Hardy/Photo
Researchers, Inc., p. 15; © Laura Westlund/Independent Picture Service, p. 16; © Belinda Images/
SuperStock, p. 18; © beyond foto/Getty Images, p. 20; © Ron Miller, pp. 21, 34; © IndexStock/
SuperStock, p. 22; © Royal Observatory, Edinburgh/Photo Researchers, Inc., p. 23; © Lionel Bret/
Photo Researchers, Inc., p. 24; © Science & Society/SuperStock, p. 25; NASA/MSFC, pp. 26,
29; X-ray: NASA/CXC/MIT/C. Canizares, M. Nowak; Optical: NASA/STScI, p. 28; © Apic/Hulton
Archives/Getty Images, p. 30; © MPI/Archive Photos/Getty Images, p. 31 (top); © Mary Evans
Picture Library/The Image Works, p. 31 (bottom); © Paul Fleet/Dreamstime.com, p. 32; © European
Space Agency (C. Carreau), p. 33; © David Nunuk/Photo Researchers, Inc., p. 35; NASA/KSC, p. 36;
NASA/JPL, p. 37.
Front cover: © Science Source/Photo Researchers, Inc.

Main body text set in Adrianna Regular 14/20
Typeface provided by Chank